I Love Shelties
ANNUAL 2021

Tecassia PUBLISHING

Published in 2020 by

Tecassia Publishing
Building 31186,
PO Box 6945,
London,
W1A 6US
www.tecassia.com

ISBN

Hardback 978-1-913916-03-9
Paperback 978-1-913916-04-6

Also available as an e-book 978-1-913916-02-2

Designed by Camilla Fellas Arnold

Dedication

To everyone that has ever had their heart captured by a
Sheltie, you know there is nothing quite like Sheltie love.

To all the beautiful Shelties we've loved, lost and those
Shelties that have come along since and healed our hearts.

To my Grandad who introduced me to the wonder that is the
Shetland Sheepdog and to my Mum that has shared my love
and journey with our fluffiest of best friends.

A portion of the proceeds of this book will be donated to
Shetland Sheepdog Welfare and Rescue, co-ordinated by the
English Shetland Sheepdog Club.

Table of

Contents

Shelties by the Sea

HOW ONE SEVEN YEAR OLD'S DREAM OF HAVING A DOGGIE BEST FRIEND GREW INTO THIS BOOK!

My name is Camilla and I live in Norfolk, UK with my husband and two shelties. Much as I loved where I lived growing up – two minutes from the beach! – the fact that I was an only child could be lonely at times. I was lucky enough to live next door to my maternal grandparents and we shared a garden that I can only describe as magical but I had to learn to entertain myself early on. I lost myself in worlds of My Beautiful Horses and Puppy In My Pocket and our family had a fair few pet cats, dogs and fish so I had plenty to occupy myself with and my childhood was happy.

Then my parents and I moved and things began to change. We did not live too far away but I didn't have a big garden to explore as we'd moved to a town. The house we lived in felt vast with its high ceilings and large rooms – too many in fact for only three people. Loneliness started to creep in as I found myself away from everything and everyone familiar. It was only a few months later at the age of seven when I found myself having to understand what it meant to have your parents divorce. Suddenly there was two of us in this vacuum of a house.

My grandad took his Border Collie to obedience classes every week and over the years I'd watched and visited. It looked like fun so I had an idea. I don't remember the conversation but my mum recollects that I went up to her one day and asked if I could have a puppy as my 'best friend' that I could take to obedience classes. I imagine it came as quite a surprise because although we had both grown up around dogs our entire lives, we'd never actually owned a dog. I didn't even know what kind of dog I wanted!

'I'll think about it,' she said to me. Thirty minutes

Camilla as a child with grandad and his dogs in his garden.

later, which is the amount of time a seven-year-old thought was sufficient to think, I breezed back and asked if she had decided whether I could have a puppy or not. 'I haven't thought about it yet!' Off I went. Thirty minutes later I was back. After doing this a few times I got the message that this was a 'big decision' and I needed to leave it longer so I dropped the subject and waited.

My mum recounts often how she spoke to my grandad about it later saying, 'you'll never guess what Camilla has asked for!' My grandad with his practical, level-headedness, immediately knew what I needed in a dog; small as I was only seven, pretty to match me, the apple of his eye and intelligent as I wanted to do obedience.

'I know just the dog!' he exclaimed.

'What's that?' my mum asked.

'A Sheltie. Like Lassie from the movie but smaller.'

Let me tell you, the minute I heard those words,

I was sold. I loved the Lassie movies. I didn't question it any further. That was exactly what I wanted.

But this was back in 1997 before Google even existed. My mum went on a search for a Sheltie, looking through newspaper adverts, calling numbers, visiting pet shops. She managed to reserve one down in London (a three-hour drive for us) when my nan happened to mention it in a local pet shop. The shop owner then announced she knew of a litter being born locally.

My mum rang to find the puppies had only just been born. There had been three but one had died leaving two bitches. We arranged to visit at the weekend.

All I remember was a long chat with the elderly couple followed by being allowed to go see the puppies and their mum in their den with my grandad's supervision. Being the first visitors, we were allowed to pick the one we wanted. They didn't look much like the majestic Lassie on TV to me, with their slicked-down fur and closed eyes. I didn't know what I was looking at so when my grandad said, 'that one looks nice with the white round its neck'. I immediately agreed. He judged at obedience shows so I figured he'd seen enough to know what he was talking about. We visited every weekend after that. It was so exciting to see my puppy grow. I couldn't believe she was going to be mine!

Between my asking for a puppy and actually bringing her home, a lot of things changed. For a start, my mum and I moved back to live next door to my grandparents. I also started visiting my dad on Sundays and it was one such day when hetook me shopping one Sunday to get some of the basics for the puppy.. I chose a green tartan collar and matching lead. A family friend then asked what I was going to call my puppy. 'Well, Lassie of course!' I said like it was the most obvious thing in the world.And so it was that sometime late June, Lassie finally came home to live with us. At that moment, nothing else mattered. I had my best friend in the world. She was a clever girl and eager to please so we flew through obedience training, doing some of the Kennel Club's Good Citizen award scheme and a road safety test.

Above: Lassie and her best friend Zakey
Top: Camilla and Lassie (*Lady Clara at Jamiri*)

We started going to fun dog shows and I won a trophy for junior handling. Every weekend was spent with my mum, nan, grandad, their Border Collie Zakey and Lassie, either at a fun dog show, obedience show or on the boat my mum had bought on a whim. I was having the time of my life. In total we won 49 rosettes and two trophies at shows.

But we never managed to progress at obedience shows for one simple reason… Lassie always did whatever Lassie wanted to do and it wasn't always what you wanted her to do! On walks, she would take her own path, cheekily looking over at you before scurrying off. She would grab onto Zakey's tail as he ran after his ball and get flung around without a care in the world. And she simply would not do a recall! I remember week after week in my obedience class. I would get her to sit on my left. I told her to wait and I walked off. Turned around and called, 'Lassie come!' Nothing.

I'd tell her to wait and run at top speed and call her. Nothing. I'd be crouching down on the floor with toys and treats…. Nothing!

She'd be sitting there watching me, in her ladylike manner with what felt like complete bemusement. We tried everything but she was not interested in the slightest. She had a mind of her own.

Over the years I started to collect sheltie paraphernalia. If it had a sheltie on it, I had to have it. Not that there was much to be found! I had all the books too but found that many were older and going out of print.

It was frustrating to me, knowing how wonderful this breed was, but realising that hardly anyone else knew about them. During school, I found out I was good at graphic design and I'd always had a penchant for writing. I would say to my mum that it would be amazing to write sheltie books one day when I was older. I didn't know how, but I knew I wanted to do it.

We lost Lassie in November 2007 after an 18 month battle with bowel cancer. It hit me so hard to lose my childhood best friend and I found I couldn't bear to look at her photos because I missed her so much.

Camilla and Carly
(Allington Pippins Lady)

Nearly a year later, one Sunday morning, I remember the feeling of missing Lassie hit me like a punch in the stomach. I cried to my mum and asked if she had ever wanted another dog after Lassie. The moment she said yes, it felt like a weight had been lifted. We never questioned whether we should get a different breed. It was an unspoken given. There was something about the Sheltie that had reeled us in and there was no going back!

One morning I got a phone call from my mum while she was at work. She'd been reading adverts in a newspaper and seen there was Shelties for sale. It was the day Lassie had been gone for a year. I wrote down the number and ran to tell my grandad. Before I'd even finished speaking, he was on the phone and had reserved the only sable girl in the litter.

I like to think that Lassie sent Carly to us. Not only did my mum spot the advert exactly a year to the day after we lost Lassie, but we found that they both had Lady in their pedigree names. Carly's dad was called Teddy. We'd always called Lassie our teddy bear. It felt meant to be.

Carly came to live with us on a cold December day. I started university that year so I was lucky to have a long winter break which was the perfect time to get to know the feisty little rascal we brought home. She was the smallest of the litter but always made sure her presence was known. I knew by that point that Shelties were always going to be part of my life so I knew that anyone I met had to not only like them but had to be approved by them too! Carly had been quite frightened of one of my previous boyfriend's so I was keen that any future suitors made her approval. I need not have worried.

I had my first date with my now-husband in a coffee shop in our

local city. It was love at first sight for us both. I didn't have a car at the time so was being picked up by my mum. He walked me back to the car, keen to stay in my company as long as possible when the next thing we know is my mum is winding down the window saying hi and holding Carly up to say hello.

Did I mention it was love at first sight?

For Carly, it was also love at first sight. She loved my husband the moment she met him and he felt the same. Whenever he came to pick me up, he had to greet her first as she stood at the gate crying and stamping her paws in excitement.

It wasn't long before we were buying our first home together and my husband asked my mum what would happen to Carly seeing as she belonged to both of us. Her response was, 'you're taking my daughter, you can't have my dog too!' So, we moved into our new house leaving Carly at with my mum. If I thought I was lonely before, nothing prepared me for that year. With a fiancé at work all week, no car of my own and working from home, I felt like I was going crazy. I saw my family once or twice a week but with no one to talk to all day long, the days felt endless. The only thing that kept me going was planning our wedding. I remember having a discussion with my mum about what she could get us as a wedding gift. Then my mum uttered the immortal words…. 'how about a sheltie for a wedding present?'

Mia joined our family in April 2015 and quickly became my extra limb. Working from home meant we were together 24/7 so we were very attached. She was such a well-behaved puppy and flew through all the obedience because she was very clever. I decided I wanted to try agility and with her happy, easy-going nature I thought she'd enjoy it – Carly, on the other hand, would have been terrified of the equipment. What I didn't realise when we started agility was just how much we would love it. There's nothing quite like that feeling of flying around a course!

We had lots of friends and family that loved both Mia and Carly and wanted to hear about their adventures so I set up a Facebook page for them and called it *Shelties by the Sea*. I'd post little stories, updates and photos about what

Mia *(Neraklee Stardreamer)*

they were getting up to and even recorded some songs using an app that makes it look like your dog is talking which always gives everyone a laugh.

At this point, I'd graduated from university and was working as a freelance graphic and book designer. Time and time again, I entertained the idea of doing my own sheltie designs on products or writing sheltie books but it never got further than being an idea.

As Mia grew older, I realised she was more of a pack dog. She became reluctant to go on walks with just me but the minute she could go on a walk with me, Carly, my mum, auntie and my grandad's dogs, she completely lit up. Carly, on the other hand, was happy being the only dog but it bothered me that Mia was lonely. Having experienced it myself, I didn't like the thought of her being unhappy and bored even though I was at home, I still had to work and couldn't pay her constant attention so I had an idea…

You guessed it, how about another dog?!

Teddy entered our lives in January 2019. I went with my husband and grandad to pick him up and we put him in a soft crate on the backseat. By the time I'd got into the front seat of the car, he had climbed out and curled himself up next to my grandad. I went and put him back in the crate. He wriggled and cried and slipped out of my hands to get himself sitting next to his chosen person, my grandad. He rode the entire way home (a two-hour drive) sat next to my grandad. I'd never seen such a well-behaved puppy in my life!

Teddy settled into life with us well and Mia immediately assumed the role of mothering him with gusto. She was so happy to have her own pack and despite being a high energy puppy, Teddy never got in her face. They played so lovely from day one and are very attached to one another, there's never been any jealousy or problems and it's wonderful having our little pack with Mia being a mummy's girl and Teddy is a daddy's boy. We call him our lovable rogue.

Unfortunately, 2019 was also the year we lost Carly. She had started having idiopathic seizures in August 2018. She was put on medication and had regular blood tests to check her levels and she settled for a while but then had a massive seizure in April 2019. The vets wanted to trial her on different medication at this point –the plan was a high dosage that sedated her to start with that would gradually be reduced until the balance was struck. However reducing the dosage led to a massive seizure that she never recovered from and she went to rainbow bridge in May 2019. It was a difficult year and my mum found it especially hard to be without a dog. A few weeks after losing Carly, she told me she couldn't be without a sheltie so we began the search for a puppy. We asked all the breeders and friends and eventually, a friend of ours told us she was going to a show and would speak to someone who had a litter of puppies for us. By luck, the breeder still had one left so we reserved it immediately without even seeing a picture. When we did see the picture though, we all fell in love at first sight. We had to have her in our pack.

This little sable girl lived on the other side of the country though! Luckily the breeder's sister lived between us so my mum was able to meet the breeder there, breaking up the puppy's journey to join us as Shelties by the Sea.

Talia arrived in August 2019 and for her and Teddy, it was love at first sight. Mia has found it more of a struggle because Talia is very lively but overall, they're a very happy and striking

Top left: Teddy *(Richmaus Yogi)*
Above: Talia *(Camellia Lady)*

trio when they're out and about. We've kept the *Shelties by the Sea* page up to date with their adventures and I finally decided to start exploring creating my own sheltie designs last year which felt like the realisation of a long-held dream for me: *I Love Shelties* was born!

Then late in November 2019, a friend who is a numerologist asked if I could design her book for her and if I knew anything about publishing. The conversation grew from there and suddenly I put two and two together and made four. I knew all about book publishing and it was something I'd always wanted to do! By creating my own publishing company, I could marry up so many of my skills and interests in design, writing and focusing on publishing genres that were of interest to me.

Thus, *Tecassia* was born! I thought long and hard about a name for my publishing house. I saw a lot of names were based on either the owner's names or puns on words or books but I

Above L to R: Talia, Mia and Teddy in the heather
Right: Camilla and Mia, Teddy and Talia (L to R) in 2020

didn't like either approach. I then thought back over what I truly loved and what inspired me: my dogs. I used elements of all their names to create *Tecassia*: Lassie, Carly, Mia, Teddy, Talia. I love the fact that it holds so much meaning and honours their memory. Many of the books I intend to publish will be within the personal development and spiritual genres as that is an area of great interest for me but there is one side of it that is a personal endeavour – books about shelties. There aren't enough books in the world about our wonderful breed and I want to change that! I then had the idea for this book and the rest, as they say, is history. I hope that this can become an annual tradition, bringing together sheltie lovers and owners around the world and raise money for Sheltie rescue. I hope you enjoy this book and I'd love for you to consider sending in your stories and photos for next year's edition so we can help raise the profile of our favourite breed.

With love, licks and paws,
Camilla and the Shelties By The Sea

To follow *Shelties By The Sea* visit:
www.facebook.com/sheltiesbythesea or
www.instagram.com/sheltiesbythesea

Pepsi, 8 from
Shetland, UK

Leone, 1 from
Toronto, Canada

Abby, 8 from
Kentucky, USA

Laika from Edinburgh,
Scotland

Robbie, Trushka and Tosca
from Norfolk UK

Georgia from
Massachusetts, USA

Around the world

This much is true, if you're a sheltie lover, you're a sheltie lover for life. There's something about this wonderful breed that keeps us coming back for more – and one is never enough! It's safe to say so many of you feel the same way as we've had people writing in from far and wide with their stories and photos. So here's to all of these gorgeous faces from acround the world!

Tommie, 4 years
old from Halsteren,
Netherlands

Sundanze, 5,
from Melbourne,
Australia

Haley, 8 from
Penfield, NY
USA

Keeko, 5 from
Arbroath, Scotland

Teddy-Boo 2, from
Norfolk UK

Cali, 2 from
Berkshire UK

Brothers Ziggy
and MacAllan
age 6 months
from the UK

The Hobbitpaws gang from the
Shetland Islands

Elsa and Saphie from
Norfolk, UK

Mulberry, 5 from
North London UK

Laddie 7 from Hull,
East Yorkshire, UK

Chaos, 5
from Essex,
UK

Pandora and Dice
from Newmarket
Suffolk

Roxy, 6 from
Hampshire UK

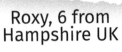

Jordie 8, Bryn 2 and Charli 17 months
from New Zealand

Dexter, Ziggie and Suni from Norfolk UK

Rosie, Bramble and Ben from Norfolk UK

Kacie Blue 7, Missy 6, and Tucker 6. Missy and Tucker are siblings from New Hampshire USA

Boo Bear 10, from North Carolina, USA

Wee Charlie and pal Keeko from Scotland

Joy with her pal Grace from the UK

Rosie 2, from the UK

Finn, Ella, Aja, and Falcon [The Sunshine State Shelties) from Florida, United States

Teddy from Kings Lynn, UK

Shoka, Simba and Kharma from Dublin, Ireland

Teddy, 5 months old from the UK

Frasier from Bournemouth UK

Aline from Hungary

The Shelties by the Sea gang from Norfolk UK

Badger's New Lease of Life

WHEN BADGER'S OWNER MOVED INTO A CARE HOME, BADGER GOT A NEW HOME AND NEW BEST FRIEND TO PLAY WITH!

Badger and his new friend Archie

We got Badger in February 2015, aged seven. We wanted an adult dog as we felt it would be better for Archie, our seven year old terrier.

We contacted Shetland Sheepdog Rescue with our details, very quickly we received an email from Badger's breeder, Hilary saying she was looking to rehome. Sadly his owner was going into care, suffering from dementia. Luckily they were about an hour away.

After several emails and phone calls, it was agreed Badger would move in with us when his owner into care. The wait felt an eternity but was probably about six weeks. I felt so sad for the owner and Badger knowing they'd both be confused.

When we collected him he'd been to the groomers, smelling lovely, looking smart. But he was wary and introverted. He'd never been upstairs before as he lived in a bungalow, so it took a while for him to get used to going up to bed! After a short time, he began to open up. He's still cautious with strangers but with us he lets his true personality shine.

He was overweight, having dined on his owners meals-on-wheels for some time. He's gone from a portly 12.5 kg to a trim 7.5 kg. He also had dental issues and had 20 teeth removed, with no adverse effects.

He's such a cheerful character, loves cuddles, food, sleeping and adventures. He's starting to slow down, showing signs of arthritis. He's got a dog pram and a backpack carrier like what toddlers are carried in. Not for everyone, but he gets to go on longer walks without overdoing it or missing out on fun with Archie.

Rescuing a Sheltie has been the best experience. We can't imagine life without Badger. He and Archie are a marvellous pairing, really bring out the best (and occasionally worst) in each other!
Lisa Johnston, UK

Lavika Kennels, How It All Began

LAVIKA IS ONE OF THE MOST SUCCESSFUL SHELTIE KENNELS IN UK TODAY

To date, Lavika Shelties have gained seven champion titles, seven junior warrants, won Best In Show many times at breed club shows, won 44 CCs [Challenge Certificates] and many RCCs [Reserve Challenge Certificates] including 2CCs, 3RCCs and 2 Best Puppy at Crufts. According to the yearly show results, the young Lavika kennel was runner-up top breeder in the UK in 2016 winning 5 CCs and 4 RCCs with four different dogs of their own breeding.

They were top breeder in the UK in 2018 winning 13 CCs and 7RCCs (including triple wins – DCC, BCC & BRCC [Dog and Bitch Challenge Certificates]) with five different dogs in one year, and runner-up top breeder in the UK in 2019 winning 7CCs and 6RCCs (including two doubles – DCC and BCC) with four different dogs. Lavika Shelties also set the record in UK show scene with the most number of own bred dogs who won CCs in the past 10 years (2010 – 2020).

They've been hugely successful since the very beginning and now Lana shares their story in her own words. Part one takes us back to the very beginning of the story in Ukraine.

I moved to the UK in 2004 and settled here in Cornwall in 2005, our affix 'Lavika' which comes from the first two letters of the names of our family at that time (**LA**na, **VI**nnie and **KA**tya) was registered with the Kennel Club in 2006. Katya is now fourteen years old and has been following in her mum's footsteps in the show ring since she was five years old. But how did it all begin?

Above: *Lana and Natalia with Tino, 2003*
Right: Elles

I was born in Ukraine in a town called Khmelnytskyi in the south-west. Together with my twin sister Natalia, we had loved animals for as long as I can remember. As children, we had guinea pigs, hamsters, fish, cats, helped our grandmothers to look after farm animals and always dreamed about having our own dog. At the age of 11, we both seriously considered getting a pet dog, exploring all the breeds and read lots of books on keeping a dog We were interested in any dog we met on the street, often following confused owners to admire their dogs! The walls in our bedroom were covered in dog pictures.

We settled on the rough collie breed and I remember I had a vision of a nice long-coated dog lying on a rug by my bed. A year later, in 1990, we bought our first rough collie, a tricolour female who we called Bagira.

One day during one of our walks, we met a young lady Galina with a lovely rough collie dog. We started chatting and found out that she was a very active collie-lover, she introduced us to the pedigree dog show world!

From that moment we devoured everything we could about the rough collies – pictures, show results, history and pedigrees worldwide. After a year we knew everything about past and present dogs, pedigrees, lines, attending shows and taking photos, famous kennels histories and top winners. We had over 100 penpals from all over the world sharing pictures, news and facts on rough collies. We were completely hooked and decided it was time for our own show dog. Galina helped us to get a sable and white puppy female from one of the top representatives of the breed in Ukraine at the time. Her pedigree included such UK lines as *Pelido, Claredawn,* and *Arranbrook*. We called her Elles. She did

very well at shows winning top awards. At that time we came up with a name for our kennel, *Lovely Funny,* which we thought were the best two words to describe our dogs.

Looking through copies of magazines, which were sent to us from abroad, we discovered shetland sheepdogs. An unknown breed to us at the time, we fell in love at the first sight. From that moment we wanted to know everything about shelties but at the time there were only a few examples of them in our country, so the search began among lines and breeders abroad.

We had in mind our dream sheltie, a tricolour dog and we were extremely lucky to find one in the German Kennel, *Vom Ohmtalteufel* of Beate and Udo Alexander. The dam was *Black Hair Lady of Golden Sunshine* (*Tery vom Locarnesse* x *Black Beauty vom Rodgauer See*) and she had been mated in Sweden to the very well-known *Ch Shelgate Lucky Devil*, who was eleven at the time of mating, bred and owned by Anna Uthorn, of the *Shelgate* kennel. Due to extreme difficulties with getting a visa to Germany from Ukraine, we faced problems collecting the pup, but, luckily, Beate and her close friend Erika Heitz were so kind and agreed to drive to Ukraine to deliver the puppy!

In June 1995 we met our German friends in Ukraine and welcomed into our home and lives our first Sheltie – the lovely Tino. We became good friends with Beate and Erika, later visiting them several times in Germany and coming full circle, twenty years later Beate bought a puppy from me, the lovely Luke, *Lavika London Look*. He is Luminary's brother and is doing extremely

Left to right: *Valentino Vom Ohmtalteufel,* Ukrainian & Russian Champion, BIS-winner in Germany 1997, Top sheltie in Ukraine 1997-2000, 2003 and 2004, Top stud dog in Ukraine 2000-2001.
Sheltie Show in Germany 1997 with Tino winning Best In Show with judges Sandra Taylor and Guy Jeavons. Photo by Martina Feldhoff.
Lana handling Tino to 1st place out of 52 entries in the Open Dog class at The Sheltie Show in Dortmund.
World Winner 2003 *Lovely Funny Glencharm Sofie.*

well, having gained his champion title and producing quality progeny in Europe today.

Tino was a very special puppy. We fell in love with him immediately and 25 years later, he still lives in our hearts. He was a handsome, intelligent, gentle, very clever dog who knew his value and enjoyed the attention. One in a million, he carried the best qualities of the breed. Tino's looks, type and even temperament were similar to his outstanding grandad *Ch Deloraine Dog Star* they were born exactly 20 years apart!

Tino exceeded all our expectations and is still currently the most titled sheltie in Ukraine. At his first show in the puppy class, he won Best in Show, it was the Collie and Sheltie Club Show in Dnepropetrovsk.

He was the first sheltie to gain the Ukrainian FCI [*Fédération Cynologique Internationale*] champion title, and top winner under such famous UK judges like Stella Clark, Terry McGowan, Duna Jones, Pauline Skyrme, Jack Wigglesworth and many more. He was top show sheltie and top stud dog in Ukraine for many years and a CAC [*Certificat d'Aptitudeau Championnat*] and CACIB [*Certificats*

d'Aptitude au Championnat International de Beauté*] winner in Ukraine, Belarus, Russia, Poland, Germany and Denmark.

His biggest victory was best in show at the Sheltie Show in Germany 1997, the largest and most popular breed show in Europe at the time. He won the open dog class out of 52 males and went on to win the best in show trophy out of 136 shelties from 10 different countries. The judges were by Mr Guy Jeavons (Grandgables kennel) and Miss Sandra Taylor (Pepperhill kennel). To start our own breeding, we imported two bitches from Germany tricolour *Black Bumblebee From Goat Valley* and blue merle *Blue Lovely Lady Vom Stormarner Land.* Both were lovely characters, successful in the show ring and breeding. Our biggest achievement was the blue merle daughter of Bumblebee – *Lovely Funny Glencharm Sofie.* She was one of three in the litter born by a Finish sire who lived in Russia at the time, *Kamajakin Asparagus,* son of *Candlebark Blue Move* and grandson of *Forestland Nutcracker.* All three siblings became champions in their countries Ukraine, Belarus and the Czech Republic. Sofie's greatest win was world winner at the World Dog Show in Dortmund 2003 judged by Jack Bispham (UK) and Sergio Lopez di Caspro (Brazil). It was an amazing achievement not just for Sofie who was only 26 months old, but for us as the breeders. We bred a limited number of litters but received many winners and champions in five colours including bi-merle and bi-colour.

Our experience with the UK Shelties started with importing two lovely males from the legendary *Landover* kennel.

Landover Big Brother. born 2001(left) and *Landover Blue Frost, Faradale* and *Ruscombe lines,* born 2002 (right).

Thanks to our dear friend Mike, a blue merle, *Landover Blue Frost* and sable and white, *Landover Big Brother* arrived in Ukraine for us. They both became champions and both proved excellent stud dogs.

Our main mission in Ukraine was not just showing, breeding and popularising shelties. We wanted to gather all sheltie lovers and spread the love, knowledge, experience, and history of the breed.

Being just two young girls, already owners and breeders of the top kennel in the country, we published four handbooks on shelties and rough collies in Ukraine which contained various articles on breeds, show results and winners, yearly show leaders and top charts. On top of that, we maintained the *Top of the Year Collie and Sheltie competition system* which listed top dog, kennels, stud dogs and brood bitches according to the show results and we voluntarily presented cups, rosettes, diplomas and prizes to all winners annually.

At the end of 2004, I moved to the UK and 2005 was the year I settled in Cornwall. Natalia stayed back in Ukraine carried on with our *Lovely Funny* kennel which was later renamed to *New Sheltie Dreams*. She actively showed, bred shelties and continued our winning ways as one of the top kennels in Europe up until she followed me in moving to the UK where she registered her own kennel.

2005 also became a special anniversary year for us as it marked ten years since we got our first sheltie which had set off a great chain of events. Thanks to our love, passion, hard work and dedication to shetland sheepdogs, we got to know the whole world and so many people in it and together we experienced and learned a lot of life lessons. To celebrate this momentous occasion, we held an event we called the *Lovely*

Funny Show! This event took place in a beautiful park by the river in our local town and saw many friends and breeds lovers travelling from far and wide to take part in the show ring competitions and various fun contests followed by a festive lunch.

It was an incredibly hot day, reaching more than 40 degrees Celsius (above 104 Fahrenheit) in the shade. Mr V. Robinson from Great Britain was invited to judge in the ring. He was my husband at the time and owner of the *Plymbox Boxers* kennel though he had previously been the owner of several shelties, including a show dog from *Monkswood* kennel. All participants received commemorative rosettes, prizes, winner's cups and gifts.

The atmosphere was amazing and we received so many gifts and well wishes for the future. It was a great way to finish my time in Ukraine and start my new life in the UK, which is a whole new era.

Lana Robinson | www.lavika.co.uk

To be continued in the I Love Shelties Annual 2022 to be released in November 2021.

Top left and right: Guests and winners of the 10 years celebration event *Lovely Funny Show*
Above: One of our Ukrainian *Collie and Sheltie Handbooks*. Each book was 152 pages in A5 format with colour and black and white photos and *CH Lovely Funny Go-Ahead Tverskaya Skazk*a, bi-merle.

Let Sleeping Shelties Lie

What was once a hardy little breed working on the rugged Shetland landscape, has become our much loved companions living it up in the comfort of our homes. And don't they live the high life! We're not entirely sure how they get into some of these positions, nor how they can be comfortable but they somehow manage it. It's been a tough year in lockdown but we're not sure if any of these pups have noticed...!

Jordie as a puppy from New Zealand

Puppy Roxy fast asleep on her pal Lily in Hampshire UK

Chaos as a puppy from Essex UK

Mulberry, 5 from North London UK

Chloe, Kelsi and Bindi from Washington USA

Willow, 5 from
Greater Manchester, UK

Shakespeare, 9 from
Maryland USA

Ash, 12 from Cambridgshire, UK

Laika, from Edinburgh UK

Bairn and Raya and
from Florida USA

Cash and Euro from Wiltshire,
UK

Cali, 2 from Berkshire UK

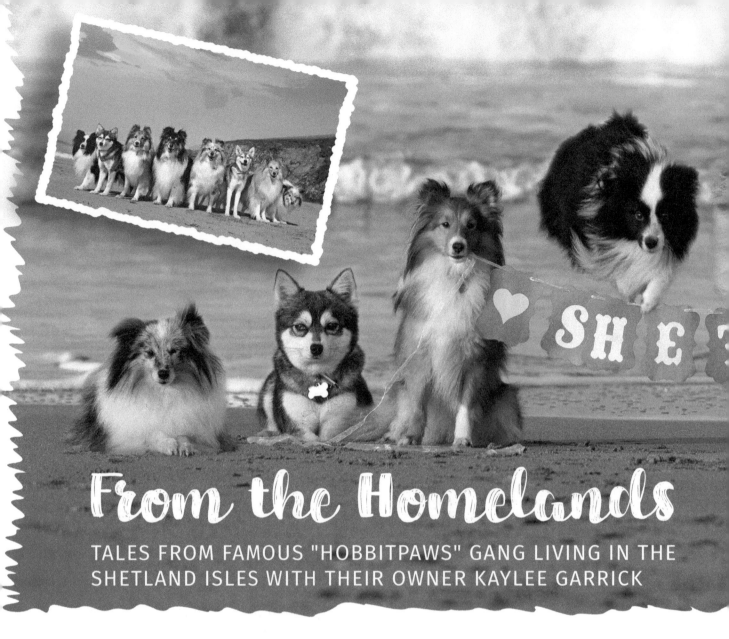

From the Homelands

TALES FROM FAMOUS "HOBBITPAWS" GANG LIVING IN THE SHETLAND ISLES WITH THEIR OWNER KAYLEE GARRICK

Swift winds sing across bitter bitten ears and folds itself around me like the hands of a dancer enticing me to move in the direction of his icy bolero. I strengthen my footing and refocus my subjects standing proud as the flurry whisks ruff of black and grey and gold untamed and free in the sea breath. A wonderful breed of contrast: as strong as the great waves crashing below; as light and agile as the small trickling streams against staggered rocks. They look so natural here against the homeland where their roots grow deep, though it is safe to say their branches have touched the hearts of many all over the world.

Bright eyes twinkle and wet noses wiggle, absorbing a hundred scents of the new day – the crisp trace of salt in the air; the sweet flavour of a passing lamb's wool; the bouquet of wildflowers swaying in a sea of green. I grab my shot in the passing moment just as the sun dips away once more behind thick cloud casting shadows across the rolling hills. Suddenly my hands feel cold without the golden light caressing them, so I take a moment to step back and warm them while I observe the scenery behind my models. The breeze is always blowing here; the scene is never still. And yet it is forever tranquil. Even against the ferocious deep blue below, moving wildly with its wide-open mouth of jagged stone teeth watching as I stand vulnerable, high atop the cliff's edge... I still feel safe. And at this moment, I cannot help but think what a privilege it is to be a part of this unique world.

Shetland is an unusual little gem lying 60° North on the map – roughly 100 miles northeast from the tip of the Scottish mainland and 200 miles west from Norway. It is made up of over one hundred small islands and is home to around 22,000 people with most originating from the main town of Lerwick. We have been a part of Scotland since 1472 after the islands were annexed as a wedding dowry for James III (King of Scotland) and Margaret of Norway (daughter of Christian I, King of Denmark). However, you would be forgiven for thinking that you were still in Scandinavia given our strange Norse accents, traditional music, old superstitions and peculiar traditions. The most famous of these customs being Up-Helly-Aa where we pay homage to our Viking ancestors by dressing up in their warrior-like regalia, marching down the streets with flaming torches and setting fire to a large dragon-headed galley ship. Day to day life here exists much the same as the rest of Scotland, although I still find myself having to explain this to some people around the world (including Scotland) who still believe we travel by horseback. Yes, we do have electricity and televisions! Yes, we have cars. No, we do not bathe in the sea, as we do have bathrooms. No, not all of us work on a croft wearing Fair Isle jumpers, I actually work for the ambulance service… no, we do not carry sheep in the back of the vehicle (that one was asked by an Aberdonian!). However, it's safe to say that working here, particularly in emergency response, poses its own unique complications.

Of course, when I'm not running around with blue lights, I spend my time taking photos of eight beautiful, rather hairy, models – a love affair with a lens which began around 20 years ago with my first dog Flint, a shaded sable sheltie. While the numbers of shelties in Shetland are now on the rise, back then to see one located within their historic homeland was rare. This is mainly due to farmers no longer using them for their original purpose of keeping livestock away from crops. Larger Scottish breeds of sheep and better fencing shifted the workload of the dog from "patrolling" an area of land to "herding" beasts into it. The taller, heavier built Border Collie soon became favourite for their increased speed and durability. The fate of the Shetland Sheepdog was then decided by the people who took them from the hard-working, often harsh life of a farm dog and cosied them up on the couch in front of the TV! The Sheltie slotted into our lives and spirits as a beloved pet very easily and what was once a hardy little breed that had evolved with the bitter winds of Shetland coursing through its veins, soon became accustomed to the feather pillows in our beds all over the world and have happily remained there ever since.

Our first boy, Flint, came from Wales. Capturing his sleek beauty against the rustic allure of Shetland's wild landscape felt easy and natural. I enjoyed doing this for 10 years before bone cancer took him so cruelly away from us. He forever left his mark on these islands where his pawprints crossed locals' hearts and inspired many to bring a Sheltie into their lives – including myself with my first one coming from the island of Burra on the West side of Shetland.

Often in the winter, conditions become so bad that our cargo ship is forced to remain stranded at dock meaning that supplies decline and shop shelves soon empty.

Most of a dog photographer's life in Shetland is spent sighing out the window at another drastically unsuitable day of wind and rain. But the main reason why I take a break from photoshoots in the winter is the lack of light. From around November to the end of February, the islands are enveloped in a thick blanket of near-constant darkness with most days having less than six hours of reasonably weak sunlight. The plus side of this is that on a crisp night, you are more likely to catch a glimpse of the glittering merry dancers sweeping across the starry sky, the northern lights. Even with eyes that have seen this bewildering and beautiful display of vibrant colours several times, I still cannot help but be entranced in awe at them.

Winters here are bitterly long and harsh with the ever-enduring winds consistently rolling in from the north, bringing with it fierce crashing waves and endless rain. But before you know it, light breaks through and a new breath of spring air floating on bird song and wildflowers finds its way to the islands. Local birds, such as our famously comical little Puffins (called "Tammie Nories" here) make their way to our southerly cliffs to nest and lambs fill the greening fields. But most notably of all, the thick scarf of winter's dark nights which had once blanketed the sky and blocked the sun is removed, transforming the islands from a land of near-constant shadow into a stretch of abiding light.

During the peak of summer, locals find themselves living through almost twenty hours of sunlight every day, which can be difficult to adjust your sleeping pattern! You will quite literally go to bed in the ever-surviving golden glow and wake up again to an already well-established luminosity sparkling against the morning tide. For most, this makes it the perfect time of year to visit the islands as the light stays with them during their many long adventures often spanning out into the middle of nowhere. When this time arrives, it is our moment to shine!

Dubbed "Burra Shelties Peerie Dollie" by the kennel club and lovingly named Fenton by me, this little tri colour started us on a wild journey which would soon have me frantically pressing the shutter button once more.

In 2016, Fenton was chosen as one of Visit Scotland's "Ambassadogs" for her outstanding contribution to encouraging Shetland tourism. She was described as "eye catchingly beautiful" by the media at the time as photos of her were plastered all over national newspapers and we were flown down to Edinburgh to meet other finalists. Since then, we have dedicated a good portion of our lives into promoting the stunning land that we live in.

This was a task that proved rather challenging at times. Shetland life is very much dictated by the weather, which is highly unpredictable at the best of times! Even in the summer months, the climate can prove to be wild and dynamically charged – much to the dismay of disgruntled, seasick tourists coming in from cruise ships.

The camera is dusted off, the props come out and we head off to create some fun photos. For those of you who don't know my hairy crew of highly professional models, I'll quickly describe you them now. I've already mentioned Fenton (tri-colour) – oldest and wisest of the group – who mentors and keeps control of the rest. Then there's Thiago (small blue merle) – people often mistake her for looking grumpy and not looking at the camera which couldn't be farther from the truth! The reality is she is the most soulful, pure, happiest little dog you could ever meet and the real reason she doesn't look forward is that, well... she can't see! She nearly lost her life at 8 weeks old and as a result, she is tiny and almost completely blind but this doesn't stop her living her life to the full!

Next is Thorin (bigger blue merle), the athletic girl who loves her flyball! Then Gimli (golden sable), the spoiled, pretty and perfect lady who travelled from France – oh la la – to be with us. Murphy (black and white) is the only boy and came from the Netherlands. He is an absolute gentleman and sweet boy to say the least. He and Gimli had a daughter who we named Jara (shaded sable). She has had a camera in front of her since the day she was born and thrives on training due to her high intelligence. We have also got two Alaskan Klee Kais – Ghost (brown eyes) and Daenerys (blue eyes) – who seem to think they're shelties and act as such! They are collectively named "Team Hobbitpaws" – due to our love of Lord of the Rings, the fact we live in a house called "Hobbiton" and it's also our KC prefix!

Our compositions commonly feature beautiful backgrounds and honestly, we are spoilt for choice when it comes to stunning locations. The islands primarily are surrounded by tall, undulating hills covered in course heather which transforms the headland into a sea of purple bloom in the autumn months. These extend out into two ways leading you towards the sea over sheer, jagged rocks of a cliff's edge; through gentle slopes, guiding you towards

soft golden sands. Shetland is famous for both from the noisy, bustling bird-filled homes of Sumburgh and dramatic scenes of Eshaness, to the serene harmony of the glittering sands of St Ninian's Isle and sapphire blues surrounding Breckon beach.

It is a fact that you cannot stand more than three miles away from the sea at any point in Shetland and if you travel to a point called "Mavis Grind" in the north, you can see both the Atlantic and the North Sea at the same time on either side of you. Our arguably most "famous" photo was taken on Minn beach – a complete fluke shot which went viral due to the fact it looked as though the entire gang were doing the "can-can"! Our local online journalism site, "ShetNews", shared the story and the rest is history.

The world fell in love with "Scotland's Most Obedient Dogs", with newspapers and TV support from across the globe sharing our

photos. The joy they were bringing inspired me to put up a display of our photos into the local hospital and I lost count of the number of emails I received after this from patients and their families thanking me and the gang for "making their time there bearable".

I often forget just how scary hospitals can be as I am in there the whole time due to my job. It was heart-warming knowing I was able to take away someone's emotional distress even for a short time.

As time went on, online recognition grew and our Facebook page "Fenton Goes Forth" developed a strong fan base of passionate dog lovers from all over. Thanks to them, we were able to start giving back to the community – raising money for charity and building awareness on important causes. Our campaign "Don't PAWS, Start CPR" helped to teach thousands of people how to perform basic life-saving skills. As a result, in 2019 Fenton and I were awarded the trophy for "Mentor of the Year" by the Ambulance Service at a large ceremony which took place in Edinburgh.

Our rainbow "PAWtraits" raised several hundred for the local MRI scanner appeal and we still donate to the Cats Protection through postcards with our photos on them sold in "The Shetland Times Bookshop" (they do make the

tourists giggle!). But our biggest achievement to date has to be the calendar, something that was asked for by fans for years and I finally decided to commit to for 2020. It was a phenomenal success and we ended up selling out in a very short amount of time! The triumph of the calendar placed me and the dogs in the national papers and television again, leading me to be interviewed live on BBC breakfast which was one of the most terrifying things I've ever had to do in my life. We were also very excited to get a mention from Lorraine Kelly on her morning show the next day!

Since then, we have worked towards the 2021 calendar in the hope that we can double our target from last year. It is safe to say that 2020 has been one of the most difficult years that many people have ever had to face. Certainly, as a clinician, it's been an extremely challenging time both mentally and physically for me. For this reason, more than ever, the money that we raise will be vital in providing support for those who need it. It is an honour to support both TASC (The Ambulance Staff Charity) and Bravehound for their amazing work in supporting war veterans and medical staff throughout the country.

It has been far from the year we had planned and while most of mine has been filled with work-related things and lockdown, a lot of the

photos we had hoped to capture haven't come to fruition; the projects we wanted to fulfil have taken a step back; the adventures we had so hoped to have could not be made. But the main thing is we are all safe and well and that's all that matters. In times like these, it is more important than ever to count your blessings and I can honestly say, we have lots of them. We have tried to make the best of it and hope our online community have all enjoyed some of the crazy videos which have come out of our lockdown experience – they certainly still make me laugh! I know for so many of you, this was meant to be the year you finally crossed the waters to visit our home – a dream come true for which many of you have waited a lifetime. And while I can't predict what the future entirely holds or where roads may twist and turn, I can certainly say one thing... when all this madness is finally over, Shetland will still be here.

The true gem of the north, standing proudly like a group of diamonds adorning the crown of Scotland. From the mysterious magic of the merry dancers to the authentic grasp of history right at your fingertips; the gentle soft sands to the scabrous serrated face of the cliffs; the tranquil days of fanciful wandering through cobbled streets to reeling the night away, burling the soles of your shoes flat in the abiding embrace of the dance; and the friendly locals in their well-composed ways transformed to those who roar the fearsome call of their Viking ancestors with a metal axe and flame banishing the long winter nights for another year.

It is a place unlike any other, pieced together with the many colourful contrasting fragments of a beautiful puzzle which fits together to create an unforgettable picture of an enchanting world. There is a peacefulness here contained within the wild and dynamically charged, untameable nature of the islands which cannot be found anywhere else in the world. But don't just take my word for it... see for yourself when you make it here. Oh, and one more thing... watch out for the trows when you do... they like to steal socks!

Here's to 2021 and a new journey ahead.

Our paths divide, people come and leave our side, laughs turn to wrinkles wide and suns set on transitioning tides.
The performance we dance on life's stage is short, Sometimes a wild waltz and sometimes hard-fought.
But add four legs to two in the tango of time, And the existence rhythm beats divine.
Our souls expand, worlds open paw in hand, tails wag and hearts understand, lights set on a brighter land.
So were someone to ask, "who'd you take to dance?",
To see these days through, my beloved dog, I'd choose you.

K. Garrick

Follow the gang at:
https://www.facebook.com/fentongoesforth

Shelties in the Snow!

There's something so magical about seeing the beautiful colours of shelties against a wintery backdrop and they love it too!

5¢ Snowballs 5¢

Top row, left to right: Charli - New Zealand, Mia - Norfolk UK,, Mulberry - North London UK, Shellee - North Carolina USA, Aline - Hungary

Middle row, left to right: Carly - Norfolk UK, Aline - Hungary, Mia & Teddy playing - Norfolk UK

Bottom row, left to right: Lucy - North Carolina USA, Teddy - USA, Onyx with pals Drifter and Skye

Top left to right: Skye and Onyx - UK, Aline - Hungary, Jordie, Bryn and Charli - New Zealand
Centre: Kelsi and Bindi - Washington USA
Bottom left to right: Mia - UK, Laika - Edinburgh UK,

The Wonderful Sheltie Community

Robbie (L) and Charlie (R)

Often when we took Robbie out for a walk so many people said, 'oh, he's beautiful, we used to have one of those years ago but you don't see many nowadays'. They were right; we hardly ever saw another sheltie.

So we posted a picture of Robbie on Facebook and asked if anyone with a sheltie would like to share a picture of their dog. We thought we might get a few replies but to our amazement, the pictures came flooding in and didn't stop!

In response, John created a group called *The Wonderful Sheltie* and the membership grew rapidly. Amazingly, it currently stands at almost 19,000 and includes members from more than 50 countries around the world. Incredible!

The Wonderful Sheltie soon became a forum where everyone shares the joy and fun that our lovely dogs give us, but we also share the sad times and tears which is inevitably the price we pay for having these beautiful shelties in our lives.

Then our world fell apart when Robbie was diagnosed with renal disease and we lost him at age six. We were heartbroken. Devastated. Nothing could ease that pain but the lovely people in his group supported us so much with their love and understanding and helped us through that terrible time. They wanted to do something to acknowledge Robbie's contribution in bringing

Top L and R: Robbie
Bottom: Charlie *'Letuck One Million'*

> ## The Wonderful Sheltie - Robbie and Friends group began simply with our pet dog Robbie and now unites people all over the world sharing our love for this amazing breed.

this wonderful community of shelties and their humans together. They raised funds in Robbie's name and we are so proud that £787 was donated to both the *English Shetland Sheepdog Club Welfare and Rescue*, and towards research into Alabama Rot at the *Royal Veterinary College, London*.

Life without Robbie felt so empty but we needed time to grieve and also felt that we needed to step back from *The Wonderful Sheltie*. After all, it was all about Robbie and he was no longer here. We handed over the control of the group to Elaine who has done a magnificent job as admin ever since. They changed the name to 'The Wonderful Sheltie – Robbie and Friends'. What an honour for our little boy!

Of course, life without a sheltie felt so empty. It was six months later that we finally felt ready to welcome our new puppy, *Letuck One Million*, aka Charlie into our lives. He was the most adorable

little puppy and of course, we had to share him with the group. Oh wow! We were not prepared for their amazing reaction. They absolutely loved him. Life felt complete again. Charlie was a happy, fun-loving, confident puppy and he was our whole world.

We become very good friends with his breeder and she encouraged us to show him. This was great fun. He did quite well and even qualified to be shown at Crufts. We were so proud! But he never got there.

A few weeks before Crufts, Charlie and John were attacked by an Akita and a German Shepherd. Charlie was just 11 months old. John had somehow managed to get Charlie away from these vicious dogs and without a doubt had saved his life, but they both suffered terrible injuries. We didn't know if Charlie would survive but our vets were incredible. We were warned he might have to have his leg amputated. He had horrendous injuries all over his body and needed five operations, including a skin

Above: Charlie's Letuck Family from L to R: Auntie Coco, sister Daisy, mummy Lilly, nana Poppy and of course, Charlie. **Top left:** Robbie. **Bottom:** Charlie

flap being taken from his tummy to cover a huge wound in his groin. He was so brave.

He allowed the vets to do what they had to do every day, sometimes without being sedated and still wagged his tail and gave nose licks afterwards. He spent his first birthday in hospital and the nurses sang 'happy birthday' to him and bought him some treats. They all loved him.

His injuries were extensive, so they borrowed a vacuum wound healing machine which they'd never tried before to help close the wounds. We visited twice a day, every day and after three weeks in hospital, that wonderful day came when we were finally allowed to take him home. But we still had a long way to go and there were many setbacks.

During all this time our Facebook friends were with us every step of the way. They shared our pain and also our joy as Charlie recovered. They sent messages, cards, toys and other gifts for Charlie. It was wonderful.

Again, they wanted to set up a fund for donations and as a result, we were able to give almost £3,500 to our vet practice to buy one of those fantastic vacuum machines which helped Charlie so much. There was also enough to buy a respiratory monitor which we're told has already saved lives. What an amazing group this is!

Charlie, now almost three, has made a full recovery, and kept all his legs! He has no pain or discomfort. His beautiful coat has grown back and now covers his many scars. He is a happy, fun-loving rascal. To our amazement, he is still as confident as he was before it all happened. He loves meeting people and still wants to play with every dog he meets, big or small. He is our hero.

The Wonderful Sheltie - Robbie and Friends began simply with our pet dog Robbie and now unites people all over the world sharing our love for this amazing breed. Robbie and Charlie have brought a smile to the faces of many thousands of people. That's quite an achievement for a couple of pet dogs. We're very proud of them both.

John and Hilary

Join The *Wonderful Sheltie - Robbie and Friends Community* by visiting: https://www.facebook.com/groups/158441637663753/

King of the Mountain

How Onyx beat the odds to conquer Mount Snowden

Onyx, our beautiful tri-coloured sheltie started to become lame at a very young age. Our local vet practice did their utmost to discover the cause and make him more comfortable but to no avail. Extensive X-rays showed nothing and pain relief didn't help. He was unable to keep up with our other sheltie and it was very sad to see him unable to enjoy the life he was accustomed to living.

By the end of September 2016, he was hardly able to walk and our local vets said there was nothing further that they could do. He was three years old. They told us they would refer us to a specialist orthopaedic surgeon.

We attended our appointment at *Fitzpatrick Referrals*, or as many people know it from the Channel 4 TV programme, *The Supervet*, in October 2016. We were hopeful Onyx could be helped but also anxious that if they couldn't help Onyx, he would have no quality of life.

Continued on next page...

I Love Shelties 21

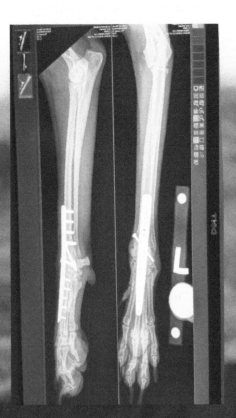

One of Onyx's X-Rays and recovering after his operation

The consultant examined him and watched him walk outside and told us he thought he knew what was going on, but would have to confirm by tests and imaging. Onyx was sedated and taken for a CT scan and other tests removing fluid from his joints.

After months of not knowing, we received an answer and diagnosis within two hours at the practice. Onyx had degenerative carpal hypertension. His ligaments in his wrist were so damaged they were unable to support him. The best news of all was that they would operate which would free him of pain, but of course, it was major surgery and there were risks.

On 31/10/16, the scariest Halloween we have ever had, Onyx underwent surgery at Fitzpatricks. His wrist was fused with what looks like Meccano and bone graft was taken from his shoulder to promote fusion to the bone and reduce the risk of failure. It was just like you see on TV!

Onyx stayed at the practice for a couple of days and they phoned us each morning with an update. He received the best care from the staff and the surgeon was amazing, who, lucky for us was at the top of his game with a head as big as his heart. All went well and we brought him home early November. Then the hard work really began!

He needed to be contained in a crate and attached to a lead and a human indoors at all times. At potty times he had to have an additional waterproof boot put on and went to into the garden on his lead. He couldn't get his leg wet due to the risk of infection. As we all know shelties like to be with their humans at all times and our shelties have always slept in the bedroom with us, so Onyx had a second crate upstairs right bedside our bed and was carried to bed every night.

To avoid any setbacks from November to January we arranged to have someone looking after Onyx around the clock, this was no mean feat with two full-time jobs and couldn't have been done without some very supportive family.

In January, he returned to Fitzpatricks for another scan and we received the good news that the operation was successful. It was healing well and he could go for short lead walks outside. Two weeks after the good news he was allowed to gradually get back to being a sheltie again!

The recovery days were tough, but it was all worth it. Onyx has never looked back. Sensing perhaps what he could have lost, he sets the pace on many an adventure up and down the UK with our other two shelties Drifter and Skye following behind him.

Photos from Onyx's climb of Mount Snowden with his pack including Drifter (sable) and Skye (blue merle)

We are now almost four years on, he's now seven years old and shows no signs of easing up. His most recent adventure was in mid-September was to tackle Mount Snowdon. He conquered the summit with ease along with our other shelties. We are so very proud of him.
Rachel Manning, UK

Super Smart Shelties

We all know Shelties are smart – in fact they are in the top ten most intelligent breeds on the planet and deservedly so! Their eagerness and willing to please nature coupled with their intelligent brains make them great at a wide range of dog sports and activities ranging from competitive sports to trick training and canicross.

We regularly see Shelties now in championship shows at agility, competing in flyball, hoopers, competitive obedience, rally-o with great results and having tons of fun at the same time.

Check out some of these smarties doing what they love!

Top row, left to right: Bryn posing on driftwood - Timaru New Zealand, Leone shaking a paw - Toronto Canada, Tosca jumping - Norfolk UK, Tali, Nellie, Eddie and Moose posing on the seesaw, taken by Megan Williams, UK

Middle row: Jamie, Ag Ch Torriglen Taking Steps Cdex Aw - Scotland UK

Bottom row, left to right: Boo Bear [blue merle] showing off his praying trick from North Carolina, USA Shoka [tricolour] taking a jump - UK, Aline [sable] playing a brain game - Hungary, Mia on the dog walk - Norfolk UK

Top row, left to right: Archie courtesy of Paws
'n' Shoot pet photography - UK, Aline bowing -
Hungary, Tali, Eddie, Moose and Nellie posing
with the weaves courtesy of Megan Williams - UK,
Tosca, Trushka and Robbie sitting on the dog walk
- Norfolk UK.

Middle row, left to right: Sam - Norfolk UK, Bryn
with pals Jordie and Charli showing off a posing
trick - Timaru New Zealand

Bottom row, left to right: Tali, Eddie, Moose and
Nellie on the A frame courtesy of Megan Williams
- UK, Rolo on dog walk courtesy of Paws 'n' Shoot
pet photography - UK,

Top row left to right: Ziggie - Norfolk UK, Mia's tunnel exit - UK, Robbie on the apex of the A fram - Norfolk UK, The Hobbitpaws gang showing off their posing tricks - Shetland Islands UK,

Centre: Tali, Eddie, Moose and Nellie posing in tunnels courtesy of Megan Williams - UK

Scotland's First Shetland Sheepdog Agility Champion

JAMIE - AG CH TORRIGLEN TAKING STEPS CDEX AW.
29/05/1994 - 23/08/2005.

Jamie was my soulmate, my homebred champion both in title and in so many other ways. He excelled in everything he did across four disciplines. Not only a super showman, having many BOB [Best of Breed] awards in beauty and Crufts qualified but also competed in working trials qualifying CDex [Companion Dog Excellent] and winning the stake.

He competed in obedience, representing Scotland twice in the Crufts inter-regional obedience teams, on the second occasion winning his class which was a wonderful experience. However, he was undoubtedly better known on the agility circuit where he dominated the Scottish mini-classes for several years.

Jamie was the winner of the very first UK agility challenge certificate under the legend Mary Ray but a plethora of near misses in the form of wins with 5 faults, reserve CCs [Challenge Certificates] and time out of competing with a serious eye injury meant we waited four years for the second CC, the judge this time was Mr Gordon Barnett of Aberdeen. Conditions were tough with heavy rain and during a thunderstorm, we ploughed through the mud after the standard dogs had already run the course, such as the weather can be in Scotland in May!

His third CC came as a complete contrast three months later in the blazing August heat (yes it did happen that year in Scotland!) Last to run in the final, he took his title under judge Peter Elms. At the grand age of 11 he became the first Scottish Shetland Sheepdog agility champion and to this day remains the only one.

Louise Saunders

Jamie – *Ag CH Torriglen Taking Steps CDex AW* with his
champion agility certificate from The Kennel Club UK

The Amazing Archie

WITH HIS LUST FOR LIFE, ARCHIE WAS STILL COMPETING IN AGILITY AT AGE 12 WITH THROAT CANCER

Left: Archie (*Reubicia Midnight Charmer*) doing what he loved, photo courtesy of Glynn Davies photography

Above: Archie and Rolo (*Butterwell Ring of Gold*) tackling the A-Frame together

Archie was born in July 2007 and he started agility in 2009 at the age of two. At first, he was a little devil going to see other dogs and running out the ring. We started competing in 2011 and did quite well getting placed 3rd and having a couple of clear rounds but I tore knee ligaments in October that year so we had to stop training and competing.

It was a long convalescence but in May 2014 we were able to start training at Quintor agility in Devon. Once again, Archie really took to it although if I was not quick enough to direct him or went wrong on the course he would run out the ring again.

He finally won into grade two in March 2016 winning both agility and jumping at Wadebridge, Cornwall, having previously won his first jumping in August 2015 at Devon Dogs. My other sheltie Rolo started also agility in 2016 at aged two. By this time I had gained a lot of agility handling skills and Rolo won into grade three in September the same year.

Archie and Rolo's best results happened in 2018 at the Roseland show in August. Both won their agility classes. I couldn't have been prouder that both my dogs were now grade four.

We started well in 2019 with Rolo placing 4th at the Kernow show. Archie at nearly 12 years old was getting consistent clears but he was slower as his age against him. His last show before his cancer diagnosis saw him come 7th out of 42 in a jumping class in July. He showed no signs of being ill and was happily running courses.

He had an operation for tonsil cancer removal and mouth cancer in August 2019. He bounced back with a clear round in anysize competition in October last year [2019]. His final competition was December 2019 at our local club where he went clear twice. We had to put him to rest at the beginning of March 2020 as his liver was struggling due to cancer spread. He was amazing. Frustrating to run, a real joker and

Clockwise from top left: Archie on the dog walk courtesy of Paws 'n' Shoot pet photography. Above: Archie with his last clear rosette age 12. Below: Julie with Rolo, Bernie (*Mohnesee Mr Bernie Black*) and her Welsh Springer Spaniel and left: Rolo aged 4 and Archie aged 11, winning small and medium agility at the Cornwall Show 2018.

stubborn but on his game, he was brilliant and loved life and his agility.

He has left a massive hole in my life but I still have Rolo, a new tricolour sheltie, Bernie who has all of Archie's lust for life and a Welsh Springer Spaniel that I hope to compete with soon. Rolo has had a couple of clear rounds this year so we have hope for him next year as he is only six years old. I loved Archie and will miss him always. He was my first Sheltie and because of him I now have my third boy Bernie – hopefully, a superstar in the making.

Julie Knee, Torquay, UK

Golden Oldies

Shelties are majestic at any age but they certainly don't stay with us long enough. Let's celebrate these gorgeous senior shelties that are still living life to the full, extra white furs and all!

Angel, 12 years old from the United Kingdom

← Flash, 14 years old from Shetland, United Kingdom

Teddy, 10.5 from Minnesota USA

Ash, 12 from Cambridgeshire, United Kindgom

Good Citizen Pepper!

Pepper is now 11 years old. When he was younger I entered him in obedience shows and in 2014 he qualified for Crufts to take part in the 2015 Good Citizens Dog Scheme Special Pre-Beginners Obedience Stakes. Although we didn't get placed, he did me proud. It was *me* who let him down. Here he is doing the 'down' stay, waiting to be called on the 'recall' and getting ready to go in the ring.
Barbara Slack

Well done Pepper, we hope you're enjoying your retirement now!

Pepper, 11 from the United Kingdom

Resilient Wee Charlie

Charlie is such a special boy to us as he has overcome so much. His first two years of life were very traumatic. At 14 weeks old Charlie broke his front left leg which had to be plated and screwed leaving him crate-bound for six months. This was so difficult for him as, after all, he was just a puppy and wanted to play, it was heartbreaking. But we knew we had to make sure he had the best recovery time possible.

At this point, he had missed out on the most important time for a puppy to be socialised and training. We took Charlie to 'Life Skills Training Classes' and luckily he came on in leaps and bounds. We were so proud of him. Life was good and there to be enjoyed.

But at 18 months old disaster struck again when Charlie sadly broke the same leg again. He broke the leg below the plate from his previous injury on the day we all arrived in Orkney for our two week holiday. We rushed him to the veterinary

hospital in Kirkwall at 3 am where our worst fears were confirmed. He was made comfortable and was due to get an x-ray first thing the next morning. We were devastated to hear from the vet that Charlie could lose his leg.

We made the decision that we were going back home to see our usual vet so we got our ferry tickets changed, telephoned our own vet to let them know what had happened and when we would arrive. We were so lucky to have a fantastic orthopaedic surgeon and he was able to save Charlie's leg. Once again his leg was plated and screwed and he was crate bound for six months to recover. He had to have the plate removed early before the six months were up as it was causing some bone irritation but he did heal nicely.

We all finally started to enjoy life again when suddenly, Charlie was unfortunately attacked by another dog that resulted in three puncture wounds that needed to be stapled. This left him not only with the physical scars to heal from but mental scars too. To this day, he is still wary of some dogs. It is only natural after such a terrible thing to have happened to him.

So you see we are super proud of our wee boy! He has gone through so much at the beginning of his life. Luckily he just took it all in his stride and dealt with it, that is just the way Charlie is with life! He is one tough, resilient, wee sheltie.

Now he enjoys life to the max; having frisbee fun on the beach, adventures up in the Scottish Glens and even attending Agility Classes which is something we thought he would never be able to do. That is why we love him so much and love to share all his wonderful adventures with his friends around the world. Our boy, the famous 'wee Charlie'.

Linda Bolt

Sheltie Smiles!

Shelties are so expressive in their faces which is another thing we love about the breed. Not only do they have a wonderful temperament but check out some of these gorgeous smiles!

Charli, 17 months from New Zealand

Boone Brown 9, from Florida USA

Aline 6, from Hungary

Teddy-Boo from Norfolk, UK

Mulberry, 5 from North London UK

Trushka from
Norfolk UK

Willow (left) and
Barney (right),
from the UK

Leone, 1 from Toronto
Canada

Cali, 2 from
Berkshire UK

Jordie, 8 from
New Zealand

Tommie, 4 years old from
Halsteren, Netherlands

Frasier from Bournemouth UK

Bryn as a puppy from New Zealand

Roxy, 6 from Hampshire UK

Laddie 7 from Hull, East Yorkshire, UK

Teddy 2, from Norfolk UK

Five Colours of Teal

AT THE AGE OF SIX, TEAL IS
ALREADY AN AGILITY CHAMPION!

Teal is a six-year old bi-black Shetland sheepdog who was bred at the 'of the five colors' kennel in Belgium. His full kennel name may well be the longest one on the kennel club register; *Agility Champion New Illusions Bi Enchantment of the Five Colors*!

Teal came to live with me in England at 12 weeks of age and I took the first 4 months off work completely in order to socialise and train him appropriately. We spent a lot of time visiting different places together to make sure he felt comfortable in all kinds of environments, trick training and generally having fun, forming a really good bond.

Right from the start, Teal showed me that he had inherited characteristics from both of his parents, a complete clown like his mother but

> Teal... inherited characteristics from both of his parents, a complete clown like his mother but a deadly serious work ethic from his father.

a deadly serious work ethic from his father. He loves to learn and had all the energy and drive I had ever dreamed of in a dog but at the same time is able to switch off at home and gives some of the best canine cuddles I have ever experienced! He is my constant shadow. He comes to work with me every day and we have barely spent a day apart since he came home. I have taught him some of the task work that the assistance dogs I work with perform, so at home he is often found loading or unloading the washing machine and fetching my slippers and the post!

Teal has been competing in agility for three years and in that time we have achieved some of my life long dreams together. He has competed at Crufts for three years running, winning the

ABC event twice, the British Open twice, runner up in the Crufts Singles and the team event and achieving my biggest dream of winning the championship event in 2019. He gained the title 'agility champion' after only three months at that level and has eight championship tickets in total.

He has won the Discover Dogs ABC semi-final twice and the British Open semi-final at the International Agility Festival three times which were both qualifiers for Crufts. He has competed that the UKA grand finals twice, winning the Masters event there and the K9 Massage Guild Challenge. He has competed as part of Team GB for three years running at both the European Open (Italy, Austria and Netherlands) and the FCI World Championships (the Czech Republic, Sweden and Finland). In 2018 he won the qualifying agility round at the European Open championships which was a huge achievement that we will both remember forever!

Teal is truly a dream dog and I feel like the luckiest person alive spending each day with him and I am blessed each time I get to step to the start line with him.

Hayley Telling

Apricot the Super Sheltie

A SUPER SHELTIES STORY

Apricot

The brave little pup
who broke her leg

On Sale Jan 2021

Apricot, the little Tasmanian devil as her owner Natalia calls her, is just like any other cheeky puppy. She likes to bite feet, eat shoes and have fun exploring the world. Except Apricot is not like any other puppy. After being born from a much longed for litter, the family soon found that accidents happen when you least expect it and the little pup found herself having to cope with a leg broken in two places at the tender age of 11 weeks old. Luckily through the dedicated care of veterinary surgeons, her family and her strength of character, Apricot fought on and her inspiring short story will be released as an ebook in January 2021.

**Sign up to the Tecassia newsletter at www.tecassia.com/newsletter
to be notified of the release date!**

Special Shelties

So many of you wrote in with incredible stories and photos and we've done our best to include as many as possible in all the different sections of the book. We had a few submissions that were special in their own right and we wanted to honour these truly special shelties – from the first ever owned which started a true love of the breed to the most sweet and special personality, here are our top picks of some extraordinary little shelties!

Left: Christa and **right:** Jaz both owned by Glynis Smith

Tina was Pam Marshall's first Sheltie, born in 1975.

Christa was my third Sheltie, she came along as a buy one get one free addition. My second Sheltie, Sam, suffered SA and at five months his breeder brought Christa, aged eight, to us for a week to see if being with an older dog would help him. It worked like a dream and Christa ended up staying until she crossed the bridge in 2015.

Christa was the most laid back, happy little soul you could ever meet. Her tail wagged for anyone willing to give her attention. She was in charge in the household, especially when number three came along four years later.

She loved being in the garden, relaxing in the sun and watching over her two youngsters. This picture was taken in the garden just months before she left us. My Springtime Christabelle.

Jaz was my first Sheltie. I'd wanted a Sheltie for many years but the opportunity never arose until 2001 when I was no longer working and the children were older.

Pups were hard to come by but I was given the name of a breeder who had one male pup left. We drove for a couple of hours to meet the youngster and it was love at first sight. He was adorable. After a good while with the breeder and meeting all her other dogs we finally drove home with this gorgeous bundle of fluff. For the entire journey he had his little front feet on my chest staring at my face, this was the start of the most wonderful relationship between this beautiful dog and myself, although it was only to last eight short years. He was my world and for the rest of my life my little Jaz will always be number one.

Glynis Smith - Norfolk UK

Sheltie Celebrations!

Shelties love to be part of all the activity of their households due to their busy and curious nature. Their eagerness to please and intelligence make them quick to learn to pose (for treats of course!) which can make some amazing photos as you've seen from Kaylee and the Hobbitpaws gang on page 22. Take a look at some more shelties from around the world having their own celebrations!

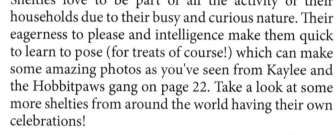

Clockwise from top left: Dex, 11 from California, USA is so happy and excited about his homemade birthday cupcakes!

Leone from Toronto, Canada celebrating his first birthday

Charlie and Minty celebrate their birthday

Teddy, Mia and Talia celebrating Talia's first birthday at a Doggie Diner in Cromer UK

Left to right: Finn, Ella, Aja, Circa and Falcon celebrating
Independence Day (4th July) in the United States

The Hobbitpaws gang celebrating Halloween on the
Shetland Islands as ghostbusters!

Aline from Hungary loves to dress up! Here's some of her looks to celebrate Halloween and Easter.

Carly and Mia from Norfolk UK at their pawrents wedding

Willow, 5 from Greater Manchester, UK celebrating her pawrent's wedding

The Sunshine State Shelties creating an autumnal wreath to celebrate autumn

Shelties by the Sea and pals Rosie, Bramble and Ben celebrating autumn in the pumpkins and leaves

"Santa baby, just slip a Sheltie, under the tree FOR ME."

Top: Aline from Hungary
Left: Teddy from the USA

Clockwise from top left: The Sunshine State Shelties from Florida.

Willow, 5 from Greater Manchester, UK

Joy 2 from the UK

Gracie 8, from North Carolina USA

Sky, Fudge and Buddy from the UK,

Mia and Teddy from Norfolk UK,

Teddy from the USA

The Skies the Limit for the Longrange Kennel!

The Longrange Kennel have had some tremendous placements in the past year with the beautiful Skye becoming the Czech Republic's top sheltie of 2019, Monty becoming a Junior Russian Champion and Luca receiving 4th place reserve at Crufts 2020 and a Junior Warrant. Congratulations on those amazing results!

Right: Skye, *Longrange Skies The Limit*
Bottom right: Luca, *Adventurine Bohemia Classic Joins Oakcroft*
Bottom left: Monty, *Adamant Bohemia Classic*

The Sheltie Blogger

FIND OUT HOW NEW ZEALANDER BECKY CAME TO BUILD THE WELL-KNOWN SHELTIE PLANET WEBSITE

Becky and Piper

Piper and Howard

My name is Becky. I'm a New Zealand based writer with a passion for animals. I started blogging about Shelties in 2008 after falling in love with a puppy named Howard. Since then, I've also fallen head over heels with his brother, Piper. Together they are the fluffiest, noisiest, cutest, silliest dogs in town. These two devastatingly handsome Shelties are incredibly sweet, you have to agree.

We discovered Howard Woofington Moon as a puppy when he was 8 weeks old. Despite his timid first appearance (he was only a baby after all), he turned out to be a rather bold, proud, confident grown-up Sheltie.

Somewhat unusually for a Sheltie, Howard loves strangers. He bounds up to everyone on our beach walks to say hello. He doesn't mind if you're sunbathing. He'll take time out of his busy schedule to block your light and sniff your bum. Of course, you don't mind. You're having the honour of meeting Howard!

At night, Howard turns his affections to us and becomes one smoochy devil of a dog. He enjoys snuggling up with us on the couch and in bed. Yes, IN bed.

Piper moved into our house when he was nine months old, after responding to a flatmate wanted ad in the local paper. Although our advert specified a 30-something professional with at least three references, we made do with the fact that he was toilet trained. Piper was an immediate hit and turned out to be an especially affectionate and loyal adult Sheltie. All in all, Piper is the more typical personality you'd expect of a Shetland Sheepdog, known for their sensitivity and eagerness to please.

In fact, Piper follows me everywhere he possibly can. He's very doting, and never hesitates to lick the toe-based wounds of our house guests while they try to relax on the couch and hold a conversation. Yes, Piper is the sweetest, loveliest, timidest, silliest dog in the world and will nibble the toes of anyone who disagrees.

Since we live in New Zealand, we have the pleasure of going on many outdoor adventures. Beaches, coastlines, forests, parks, Mount Doom, you name it. No, maybe not Mount Doom. But definitely some very large hills and the occasional escarpment.

True, these dogs have been around the block and even followed us overseas when life got really crazy. They're now back in Auckland, living out their old age in what must be one of the most beautiful places in the world.Besides writing about Shelties, I'm studying a Bachelor of Science in Zoology, which covers many aspects of Animals: Behavior, Classification, Development and Evolution (ABCDE for short). This will one day enable me to be a science writer. I'm developing the illustrated blog Science Me in the meantime. Take a look – it has cartoons!

Before I met Shelties, I'd always had a strange relationship with dogs. We'd had a family dog when I was a kid; a sweet little Poodle mix called Penny. But I was also afraid of dogs: their behaviour confused and scared me. Why did dogs wag their tails? Why did they slobber? Why did they

> *I set my heart on adopting a Sheltie but it turned out they're hard to find in New Zealand. There were no rescues at all.*

jump up at me? Why did they scratch and bite? At the same time, I thought some dogs were just really beautiful and amazing. I'd watched the Labyrinth a hundred times and wanted an Old English Sheepdog just like Sarah. Fast-forward 15 years...

I had just emigrated to New Zealand. My partner Pete and I moved into our first house together. And we finally had the opportunity to get a dog of our own. I researched lots of dog breeds. Big dogs were out. Too scary, I thought. And too big for our landlord to agree to it. So a small dog it was. And that led me straight to the magnificent Sheltie.

I set my heart on adopting a Sheltie but it turned out they're hard to find in New Zealand. There were no rescues at all. Eventually, I had a stroke of luck.

The two grand old woofies

I found a Sheltie breeder in Papakura called Shelton Shelties who happened to be homing a litter of Sheltie puppies the next week. I was over the moon! But that was short-lived because the breeder told me that all of those puppies were destined for other homes. People had signed up for them months ago. Perhaps it just wasn't meant to be. We had even started looking for a Rough Collie to adopt when I got a call. It was the Sheltie breeder. One of her buyers had fallen down the stairs and wrecked her ankle. It meant she wasn't ready for a puppy right now. And just like that, 'Toes' was ours if we still wanted him. That's how we met this gorgeous little guy.

The breeder had nicknamed him Toes because he had little white socks on each paw. Later that day we decided to give him the modest name of Howard Woofington Moon.

Howard didn't leave my side for the next three days straight. He was clearly a scared and vulnerable little puppy having been parted from his litter. I stayed with him day and night. As he settled in, he started to grow bold and curious. Howard trotted around exploring his new house and all its strange objects. He played with lemons in the garden, pulling them off the tree. And he met lots of new people. Everyone wanted to meet our new Sheltie puppy.

Soon, we started taking Howard for daily walks along the beach. Even as a tiny puppy, he loved to bound up to much bigger dogs. And he didn't hesitate to run up

Howard as a puppy

to strangers to say hello. This was definitely not the shy Sheltie that is common for this breed. Howard rapidly grew into a very confident adult Sheltie and by one-year-old, he was full size.

Today, Howard is 11 years old. It is shocking how time flies. Of course, I still think of him as my cheeky little Sheltie puppy and I'm sure I always will.

Along Came Piper

Back when Howard was nine months old, I emailed his breeder with some up-to-date photos. I mentioned in passing that we would love to have another Sheltie someday. I didn't expect her to call five minutes later and offer us Howard's brother.

I learned that the breeder had reserved one of her puppies to be a show dog. He was eager to please but also nervous, Piper wasn't going to handle the show dog lifestyle at all. He needed a loving family where he could feel secure. Who better to live with than his brother? We mulled it over but deep down we already knew the answer...

Since they were half brothers, I was expecting to meet a dog very similar to Howard Woofington Moon. I had a vision of him looking just like Howard but wearing denim dungarees for some unfathomable reason. But the moment I laid eyes on Piper, I realized he was completely different to our bold and confident boy.

When Piper caught sight of us, he crouched into a tiny ball like a hedgehog. Terrified and anxious, he tried to melt himself into the grass so we wouldn't see him. Howard, on the other hand, was busy peeing on the breeder's foot.

We introduced the boys and they sniffed at each other curiously. From then we knew they'd get along. We took a tour of the Sheltie kennels and met their father, Storm, who looked strikingly like Howard. We met a dozen other beautiful Shelties that day. By then I was Sheltie obsessed and it was a huge treat to meet so many Shetland Sheepdogs. The journey home was scary for Piper. He sat tensed up and scared on my lap. He threw up twice. I did everything I could to reassure him. I wished he could have understood but he was just so scared of everything.

Life got a lot better for Piper after that. Reunited with his brother, he settled into his new home. The timid little guy found his voice too!

Piper has a gorgeous habit of howling like a baby wolf when the answering machine goes off.

Sometimes we go on a big hike into the forest and start howling so Howard and Piper can go for it. It's a really great feeling when we all howl together.

Piper is also the perfect lap dog. You only need to make eye contact across the room and he'll immediately sit up, ears pricked, tail wagging, waiting for you to invite him up. Life with two Shelties is great.

Because both Pete and I work from home they're rarely alone, which suits sensitive dogs like Shelties. In the house, or out and about, our Shelties love to play together. Piper uses his nose to open underwear and sock drawers, and Howard uses his teeth to displace the contents around the house. It's not unusual for visitors to see Howard proudly trotting into the living room with my underpants in his mouth! But they are good dogs really. Especially when liver treats are involved.

Read the blog at: https://sheltieplanet.com
Or see Becky's Science cartoons at:
https://scienceme.com

Over Rainbow Bridge

There is never enough time spent with our precious, furry friends before we have to say goodbye. And while these have been the hardest pages to put together, it is a privilege to be able to honour these special souls that have crossed over to rainbow bridge in the last year.

For those of you still missing a beloved friend, while you may never forget or stop missing them, I hope you can find a way to heal your heart as your dear shelties would want you to find happiness again – you know how much they hate it when we get upset! So, until we meet again sweet shelties, run happy, run free.

Left to right: Maddie and Tia

I have owned five shelties in twenty five years and my last two, sisters Tia and Maddie I lost within the last twelve months. Tia, a tri-colour was rejected by her mother at birth due to her having a foot defect. I pleaded with the breeder to feed her by hand and let me give her the good life she deserved. Luckily she let me do just that and I brought her home with her sister Maddie at ten weeks old.

I nursed my husband with cancer in the first two years of their little lives and after I lost him they were my constant companions. In the eight years since my husband died, my girls filled an awful void and loneliness on my life.

Now they have gone to rainbow bridge. Tia died in my arms in October 2019 and my Maddie died in March 2020 during the Covide-19 lockdown. I never got the chance to say goodbye and to thank them for their loyalty and love over the last ten years so I honour them today in the pages of this book.

Patricia Sharkey

Buddy (above) went over rainbow bridge March 11ᵗʰ 2020 age 9 years and Fudge (above right), crossed the rainbow bridge 10ᵗʰ April 2020 age 13 years both owned by Pam Marshall

MURPHY - TORRIGLEN TRAILBLAZER AW(S)
10/04/2008 -18/01/2020

You were my absolute heart dog. My shadow. Together we enjoyed competing in beauty, obedience, working trials and agility, you were so clever.

You were so courageous in dealing with your ligament injuries. You loved your buggy as you still had the chance to enjoy our walks, you had even learned to walk again. It seemed there was no stopping you. However, when the tumour was diagnosed I knew our time was limited. I decided no more surgery, you had been through enough. You were tired, I kept you comfortable until you made it clear it was time.

I miss you every day and will never forget your final breath cradled in my arms.

Louise Saunders

Here Comes Trouble!

Shelties, what are they like?! We love them to bits but their curious nature sure gets them into a fix sometimes. Have a laugh at some of the funniest photos we received and see what this cheeky lot have been doing this year. And don't forget to keep your funniest photos to see them in next year's book!

The Sunshine Shelties were shooting their next fitness video in Florida USA

Bless you Teddy – caught mid sneeze!

Roxy and pal Lily spied on all their neighbours in Hampshire UK... or were they plotting their escape?

We hope Bryn didn't get her head stuck in New Zealand!

Talia in Norfolk UK forgot to open her eyes for all her photos!

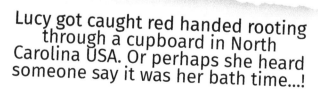

Lucy got caught red handed rooting through a cupboard in North Carolina USA. Or perhaps she heard someone say it was her bath time...!

Ash tried some sunglasses for size this summer in Cambridgeshire, UK. Looking dashing!

Heart Dogs

Heart dogs are the dogs with whom we form a one-of-a-kind, once in a lifetime relationship. There's no telling when a heart dog will arrive in your life but when they do, they hold a special place in our hearts forever. What an honour it is to hold a space for such a special soul and here we celebrate some of the wonderful heart dogs our readers have sared with us.

Top left: Sam is my second Sheltie and has been my constant companion. As a pup he was constantly up to mischief so at fifteen months of age I started agility with him to channel his energy and have some fun. I never imagined we would end up competing. Although not fast, he was my *Mr Steady and Reliable* and was just one win off grade 6 when he retired last year. He was my first agility dog who taught me so much and loved his cheese at the end of a run. Winning or not he was always a pleasure to handle.
Glynis Smith, Norfolk UK

Above: Cali saved me from the depths of depression and makes me smile and laugh every day. I love her to the moon and back, and I may be biased of course but to me she's the most beautiful dog on the planet!
Emily Mason, Berkshire UK

Left: Our Onyx (4) is a cheeky little lovebug who just loves giving full-face kisses. He will curl up at our feet and sleeps with us in bed. He is always happy with a big smile on his face and truly warms our heart. We just love him to bits!
Margaret Heart, Brisbane Australia

Left: Robbie is my soulmate, he's now 12/12 and lives with his brother's Tosca and Trushka. He is my first agility boy achieving grade 7. Our journey has been so exciting creating such a special bond, he is known as my Velcro boy as he always wanted to be by my side whilst running the agility courses. Robbie has now retired as he has developed arthritis but he still enjoys meeting up with all his agility buddies and the beautiful places we have been lucky enough to explore.
Susan Lee, Norfolk, UK

Right: This is my favorite picture of Lucy. It really shows how beautiful she is. She is funny, smart and loyal. She is my shadow, always by my side.
Vicki High, North Carolina, USA

Left: I love the shetland sheepdog's gentle nature, intelligence, and expressive face. Losing my first sheltie to kidney disease at a young age was a very difficult but I decided to get another sheltie shortly after. This photo depicts my unfiltered happiness when I got to meet my second sheltie called Leone when he was 6 weeks old.
Elmira Adeeb, Toronto, Canada

Heart Dogs

This beautiful blue merle sheltie is Angel. She is pictured here with her second litter, 'The Magnificent Seven'. She is my heart dog. Angel is now twelve and enjoying just being our family dog. She has canine cognitive disorder (doggie dementia), is losing her hearing and has arthritis and kidney disease.

Angel has seen me through the very best and very worst in the last twelve years. I was so poorly when she was two that we nearly rehomed her. I couldn't part with her though and she helped me battle through an awful time with an autoimmune disorder that is now well controlled. We decided to breed from her once I began to recover as she is so beautiful and has such a sweet nature that we wanted to share her with others without parting from her. She has made us some beautiful puppies of our own and others who found the most amazing forever families who have become our wonderful, lifelong friends.

We were truly blessed when Angel came into our family. Her daughter, Millie, (front right in the picture) and granddaughter Dory, remain in our family. We are a small family breeder team, we love shelties, that's just it. Angel gave me the best when I needed her most!

Now she is ageing it's my turn to give her the best, give her a good, loving, comfortable time and ensure that she never suffers. Without Angel, our lives would never have been so enriched. I thank my heart dog from the very bottom of my own heart!

I'm so proud of Angel, she's been my guardian angel, seen me through thick and thin. She's also been amazing with all my foster children. We've been a foster family for eight years and I have my twentieth child living with me permanently now, he is six with special needs, global day, autism, microcephaly and much more. I foster mostly sick and/or disabled children and also have had 5 mother and baby placements.

The whole time Angel has been amazingly patient living alongside some very challenging children. She's been a super nanny watching over all the babies too, including my three grandchildren.

The little tri-colour in the front left of the photo is Onyx whose tale about his treatment by Noel Fitzpatrick The Supervet is featured on page 37. Neither Rachel nor I knew that each other submitted a story to this annual. Although she lives far from me we're in touch with all our sheltie families and meet whenever we can for *Calistros* sheltie gatherings. We have the most amazing circle of sheltie friends thanks to Angel and her offspring.

Jo Austin, UK

In my lifetime I have been the proud mother of five beautiful Shelties – three of which have been heart dogs for myself and my husband. All have left me now and gone to Rainbow Bridge. But I take solace in the fact that they are not alone but all together forever.

Misty came to us in 1995 at six months old. She was beautiful, so serene and gentle. Sadly she died in 2001 at only six years old and I only have the one photo of my Misty.

We fell in love with Sophie at first sight. We brought her home at ten weeks old in 1998 as a companion for Misty. Sophie was the smallest of the litter and was able to fit into her new daddy's slipper as a tiny puppy! She feared nothing and had a little heart of a lion – she wasso sure of herself. She left us in 2010 and is so loved and missed.. Her ashes were scattered with my late husband.

Jenny was my husband's puppy and he always called her Jenny the Pup. We brought her home as a companion to Sophie after the death of Misty. At ten weeks old she was a bundle of mischief but she grew up to be so gentle. She left me in 2014 as she missed my husband after he died and nothing I did for her compensated her for his loss.

Patricia Sharkey, UK

Left to right: Misty, Sophie and Jenny

Oh my beautiful, precious Carly Pup, you have always been my heart dog. I truly fell in love with you the moment you came into my life. I fee so honoured, lucky and privileged to have had you for ten wonderful years and seven months.

I will always treasure the times we had together and our lovely walks at Cambridge, Ely, Holkam, Wells and of course, your favourite place - the woods. I have such perfect memories of you watching the squirrels in the trees. You have left your paw print in part of my heart no sheltie will ever fill. You are loved and missed beyond all words. You have left me absolutely heartbroken. You're always on my mind Carly Pup.

Jeanette Fellas, Norfolk UK

Carly

It Was Fate to be Frank!

FRANK CAME INTO LOUISA'S LIFE AT THE PERFECT TIME

Frank is super special to me. My partner and I were looking for Sheltie puppies in April of 2017 and found a pregnant sheltie die to give birth. We put out names down for a male tri-colour. Sadly, the pregnancy only produced one puppy and the breeder wanted to keep him for themselves. We were so disappointed as Shelties are not common to find.

Fast forward to August 2017 and my partner was diagnosed with terminal stage 4 cancer. He was given a few months and started some chemotherapy to try to prolong his life. Sadly he only lived six weeks and passed away on 30th September 2017.

I had never removed us from a mailing system which alerted us to new puppies being bred.One week after he died I had an alert about a puppy and near my area. I decided that taking the puppy on myself would give me a reason to carry on and get out of the house and provide another warm body and heartbeat next to me.

However, I didn't have the money to buy the puppy. I was wondering if I should put it on my credit card and worry later when the postman arrived. I opened a letter that contained a cheque for the exact amount of mo eh needed to buy the puppy. It had come from my late partner's employer and was money owed due to unused annual leave.

I immediately bought the puppy and he has been my joy and strength and constant companion ever since. He comes to work with me, licks me when I cry, plays with me, walks with me, and gives me and allows me to give, so much love.

He is my saviour and I love him more than anything. I believe he was sent to me by an angel or my partner to be exactly what I needed at exactly the right time.

Louisa Aiton, Torquay, Devon, England

Will your pup be in next year's book?

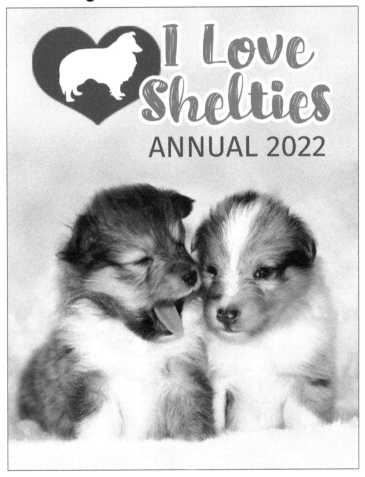

We hope you've enjoyed this book and we intend to turn this into an annual tradition for the sheltie community to celebrate this wonderful breed. Thank you to everyone that sent in photos and stories – we couldn't make this book without you! We'll be accepting submissions for next the next book in the new year and we highly recommend you sign up to the newsletter for Tecassia Publishing or follow I Love Shelties online to be the first to know when submissions open.

In the meantime, please let us know what you thought of the book by leaving a review on Amazon and send us your photos of your pups enjoying their copy!

Sign up to the Newsletter: www.tecassia.com/newsletter
Follow I Love Shelties: www.facebook.com/ilovesheltiesworldwide
Email us at: hello@iloveshelties.com

Lightning Source UK Ltd.
Milton Keynes UK
UKHW050744181120
373567UK00002B/73